Leading the Awesome

9 Steps to Facilitating an Effective Strategic Planning Session

Todd R. Christensen, MIM, MA

Stress Less Strategy Volume II

Leading the Awesome: 9 Steps to Facilitating an Effective Strategic Planning Session

Stress Less Strategic Planning Volume 2

Copyright © 2020 by Todd R. Christensen, TAWC Enterprises llc

All rights reserved. No part of this book may be reproduced or transmitted in any form or by any means without written permission from the author.

Printed in USA by TAWC Enterprises llc, Meridian, ID (208-649-4788)

4

5

Dedication

For my mentors:

For Chantal Thompson, who introduced me to - and infected me with the incurable joy found in - effective teaching and learning.

For Larry Wintersteen, whose wisdom I try to emulate and whose faith in me changed the course of my professional life.

7

Table of Contents

Chapter One: Introduction ... 12
    Meeting Leader Expectations ... 12
    Don't Lead Your Own Meeting ... 12
    Follow the Leader ... 13

Chapter Two: What Does Awesome Look Like? ... 14
    What It Means to be a Meeting Leader ... 14

Chapter Three: Starting the Awesome ... 16
    Introduction Activities ... 16
    Making Your Entrance ... 16
    Introductions or Ice Breakers? ... 17
    Establishing the Rules of Engagement ... 18
    Setting Up the Session Bike Rack ... 20
    Managing the Characters ... 20

Chapter Four: The Nine Steps to Leading the Awesome ... 24
    Step One: Documenting the Awesome ... 24
    Step Two: Prioritizing a Values Statement ... 25
    Step Three: Identifying a Mission Statement ... 28
    Step Four: Establishing a Vision Statement ... 31
    Step Five: Dividing the Vision into Annual Objectives ... 34
    Step Six: Planting SEEDS™ (SMART Goals for the 21st Century) ... 36
    Step Seven: Creating Tactical Plans ... 41
    Step Eight: Assign Accountability ... 42
    Step Nine: Implementing the System ... 43

Chapter Five: Conclusion ... 48

Appendix — 50
- Mission Statement Formula — 52
- Vision Statement Formula — 54
- Annual Objectives Formula — 56
- Planting SEEDS Checklist — 58
- Tactic Development Table — 60
- Eisenhower Decisioning Matrix — 62

About the Author — 64

11

Chapter One: Introduction

In my previous publication, *Planning for Awesome*, I presented step-by-step instructions on how to prepare for an amazing strategic planning experience while stressing less about the process. With all of those preparations in place, it is now time to pull off the awesome.

Meeting Leader Expectations

Leading a strategic planning session can be daunting, just one of many reasons why so many organizations choose to hire an outside meeting leader with experience. As the session facilitator, you will be responsible for managing the agenda discussions, managing the various personalities in the room, documenting the decision making processes, keeping the group on task while encouraging creative thinking, tracking off-agenda yet important topics, and noting assignments.

Don't Lead Your Own Meeting

That is a lot to do for one person, which is the point so many professional facilitators make when we say, "don't lead your own meeting." First of all, if you are a leader of the organization holding the planning session, you will surely want to participate fully in the session conversations. Meeting leaders "facilitate" the conversation by inviting, encouraging and drawing out participant inputs, but they do not influence session outcomes. If you are going to lead the meeting, you must focus on group management rather than on the creative thinking needed to contribute solutions and ideas.

Additionally, as a group leader, members may already look to you for answers and guidance. If you are leading the meeting, you will have a difficult time getting members to see beyond your authority. If you make a recommendation, the conversation often ends there. It is impossible to stay neutral as a meeting leader if you are also contributing ideas.

Follow the Leader

If the previous section has not dissuaded you from leading your own meeting, welcome to the next phase of *Stress Less Strategic Planning*. Each of these chapters will offer recommendations on goals and approaches to meeting leadership to make sure you have a successful and effective event. You will find the nine steps to facilitating a planning session in Chapter Four.

Chapter Two: What Does Awesome Look Like?

Leading strategic planning meetings requires a great deal of focus and energy, but with the preparation you have already put in place with *Planning for Awesome*, you are ready for the Awesome. What does that awesome look like?

- It looks like creative thinking.
- It looks like effective problem solving.
- It looks like active listening.
- It looks like relationship building.
- It looks like goal setting and coordination.
- It looks like team coaching.

Awesome and stress-less strategic planning meeting facilitation looks like a lot of different activities depending upon your point of view. It certainly requires a number of skills, most of them communication-based.

What It Means to be a Meeting Leader

The role of the meeting leader is often confused by participants and even the organization's leadership who contract with the meeting leader. Let's define what meeting facilitators are not. Facilitators:

- do not need to be subject experts in the organization's product or service;
- should not be expected to solve your organization's problems discussed during the meeting;
- are not supposed to be the center of attention;
- do not even need to have more than a cursory familiarity with the organization's industry.

Successful facilitators are experts at matching activities to meeting purposes, drawing the best ideas out of participants, redirecting attention from themselves to the group's problem solving and creative goal-setting activities, and managing personalities into a cohesive and productive team.

Chapter Three: Starting the Awesome

Once you have an inspiring reason to hold a strategic planning session and add the ongoing processes of strategic planning to your organization's culture, the following steps will help you lead your first (or next) successful, stress-less strategic planning session. The importance of the first two decisions are easily overlooked by board members and the executive team. If you want to minimize stress associated with the strategic planning experience, do not overlook their importance.

Introduction Activities

Getting your meeting started off on the right foot is indispensable to strategic planning success. "You will never have a second chance to make a first impression." This well-known phrase can be expanded to, "You will never have a chance to correct a first impression." Over time, with extra effort and a great deal of personal attention and service, you might be able to minimize the negative effects of a poor first impression, but it will always be there, available for retrieval by the other person or people at any time they feel like justifying their mistrust or their lack of confidence in you.

Make sure your first impression is full of energy, purpose, and confidence, regardless of how you may be feeling on a personal level.

Making Your Entrance

A strategic planning session is not a rock concert. You do not need blaring music and a hyped intro over a loudspeaker.

There are two trains of thought on how a meeting leader should introduce him or herself. First, if you choose to be in the room early, before the majority of participants arrive, you should take the opportunity to learn as much as possible about the various participants. Take time to speak with them one-on-one and in small groups to get to know them. Hopefully you have practiced your memory skills, because you will want to recall names, interests, and shared stories from your pre-meeting introductions throughout the planning sessions. This approach is best for situations when you are not familiar with any, or at least a majority, of the session participants.

The second option is to play the part of the mysterious guru. Such an approach is good for leading sessions with groups so large as to make it impossible to meet all of the participants. Additionally, this approach works well for organizations whose leaders have noticed major personality conflicts between many of the participants. Keeping a bit distant, emotionally speaking, from the participants protects some of the respect you have as a guest expert. This is particularly true when groups might include individuals who are known to manipulate or brown nose co-workers and executives.

Regardless of the approach, your first few sentences should never be about you. Session participants don't care who you but rather that you know who they are.

Introductions or Ice Breakers?

Few people like the idea of playing ice breaker games. Forced social interactions can turn the promise of a pleasant morning meeting into a public nightmare for many. Granted, those invited to the strategic planning sessions should be somewhat vetted to ensure their contributions will be relevant and helpful, and they should be of a certain professional character. Still, not everyone is equally comfortable sharing personal details with a group of strangers.

Don't call this first activity an ice breaker. Besides the cultural anathema associated with the term, it immediately tells the participants that any previous interactions have been cold and unproductive. Instead, call them "warm ups."

Get the participants used to contributing and voting anonymously with this quick activity:

Give each participant access to sticky notes of three different colors (ideally red, yellow and green). On the walls or on flip charts, post three descriptive personality words, such as, "opinionated," "reserved," and "easy going." Ask participants to consider their own personalities and place a sticky note under each word. The color of the sticky note should correspond to how the participants see themselves. If they are opinionated, they will place a green ("go" or "yes") sticky note underneath. If they are somewhat reserved, they might place a yellow sticker on that wall. If they do not consider themselves easy going, they would put a red ("stop" or "no") sticky note there. They may choose green or yellow or red for all three descriptive words.

The point is, by the end of the activity, participants will have introduced themselves anonymously in a non-threatening manner, and you will have a quick visual of the group's personality. If there are many green sticky notes under "opinionated," you will need to steel yourself for potential personality conflicts. If there are lots of green stickers under "reserved," you will need to get your game on to energize the group. You can use different descriptive words of your choice depending upon what information you might want to know to start off the meeting.

Establishing the Rules of Engagement

You are going to have a variety of personalities in the room, not all of whom are excited to be together with the others. One of your most important roles as meeting leader is managing the potential mayhem of this mix.

In the spirit of "An ounce of prevention is worth a pound of cure," distributing and reviewing very clear rules of engagement (aka Ground Rules) up front is a must do for any successful strategic planning meeting. Here are the nine rules I pass out in hard copy and review as a group in every session I facilitate:

1. Be fully present and engaged. Silence cell phones and other distractions. Take disruptions outside.

2. Show respect for each other's contributions, insights, suggestions, and thoughts, regardless of your opinion. Be honest, but be considerate.
3. Accord others the chance to share their thoughts without interruption. But be respectful of time limitations of each activity.
4. No ideas are bad ideas. Any idea might be adopted or might lead to additional ideas from the group. Ideas unrelated to the purposes of this discussion will be placed in the "Bike Rack" for future consideration.
5. Be open to ideas, new or old, simple or complex, tried or untried.
6. Open up the universe for all to see. There are no protected topics or programs. Expect to contribute, or you will be asked to contribute. Be confident that you are here to make a difference.
7. Expect and give confidentiality.
8. Remain focused on the organization's unique potential for good. Be unified.
9. Commit to follow up on assignments promptly and to support others in their assignments.

You are welcome to use these same rules in your sessions (with attribution, please), whether on paper or on screen.

If you are aware ahead of time of strong personalities and potential for conflict in the room, you may even consider asking the participants to sign and submit a copy of the rules. To save time in this process, you can distribute the rules electronically ahead of time or use a form (e.g. Google Forms) to distribute them with a "Agree and Submit" button at the bottom. Even with these time saving options, I would still recommend reviewing the rules at the beginning of the meeting.

Setting Up the Session Bike Rack

The Session Bike Rack is a great little tool that both keeps the discussions on point while also capturing great ideas for future consideration.

The simplest form of a bike rack is a portion of a white or black board designated as such. You may also stick a large poster paper to a wall. If you have a partner taking notes of the meeting, he or she may also have an electronic document open at all times to which to add Bike Rack ideas.

To use the Bike Rack, simply write down any idea or comment that is not directly related to the meeting agenda but deserves to be explored at a future time. Make note of the participant who shared the idea in case you need or would like additional information at a future date.

Managing the Characters

Diversity of opinion creates powerful interactions during strategic planning meetings and creative jam sessions. It leads to new ways of thinking, new approaches to problem solving, and innovation. Without differences in the way employees, managers, owners, executives and board members view the organization, its mission and the tactics required to achieve that mission, your organization will tend to stagnate and miss opportunities for growth.

When allowed to grow in meetings without check, such differences, however, can lead to anger and frustration, shutting down the idea factory that is the planning session. When a personality begins to dominate the discussion, others tend to sit back and watch, feeling their input is no longer necessary or even wanted.

When you have two or more dominating personalities in the same meeting, the potential for open conflict rises significantly. Learning to prevent conflict while directing the creativity of differing ideas is the main purpose of any meeting leader.

Keep in mind that the vocal personalities are not the only ones with the potential for creating conflict. You will need to watch for the "quietly smoldering" characters as well. Externally, they say little or nothing for long periods of time, while internally, they are burning with frustration and sometimes even contempt. Look around the group regularly and identify these personalities by finding those with their arms folded, often tightly, crisscross over their upper stomach or even the chest. In extreme cases, it will look like they are trying to hold an explosion inside from bursting out.

In such cases, you will want to help them release steam from time to time, to avoid the explosion. You might ask direct questions such as, "It looks like you are looking at this challenge from a different perspective. Could you share some of your concerns?"

Establishing the ground rules of sharing and participation is critical for minimizing conflict. When preemptive measures require active follow up, consider the following ideas for each major type of personality:

<u>The Ego</u>: This character focuses every comment and decision him or herself. Ego wants everything to be about Ego. We all have at least a little of Ego in us. When Ego goes beyond the ground rules and starts to take over the meeting, it is critical to step in to minimize the damage. Two approaches to address this include first, getting Ego to see others' points of view ("Ego, how do you think that decision might affect XYZ department?") and second, getting others more involved in the discussion so it does not become the Ego show ("Jim, Ego is making a fair point. What concerns or challenges do you think might come up when implementing this idea?")

<u>The Observer</u>: You can identify the Observer by his or her tendency to sit behind everyone else or to the side. The

Observer will not offer unsolicited input and would best be invited to participate through the initial use of Yes or No questions. Even though the Observer prefers to remain outside the discussion, he or she will generally have an important point of view that needs to be shared with and considered by the group.

The Peacemaker: Peacemakers shun conflict. The thought of disagreeing with a colleague is more unpleasant than fingernails on a chalkboard. You can identify Peacemakers by their willingness to agree with everyone's ideas. While it is not recommended to push a Peacemaker into arguments, you can help a Peacemaker participate and contribute by asking leading questions, such as, "What do you think the best argument for this idea would be?" and "What are some considerations most people might miss when looking at this problem?" Peacemakers will be more willing to share their own opinions if they can be represented as opinions of "others" or "people generally."

The Adventurer: You will note the Adventurer for the enthusiasm he or she exhibits for a new idea. Willing to try new programs and even volunteer to lead projects, the Adventurer thrives on short-term efforts and can sometimes exhibit an inability to focus for long-periods. During a strategic planning session, you will assist the Adventurer by giving him or her a variety of approaches to the same task over the length of the activity.

The Conscientious: The majority of your meeting participants will tend to fall into this category: hard working, dedicated and responsible. They tend to see their bosses and heads of other departments as the creative genii of the organization, so they resist contributing their ideas, too often dismissing them as inadequate or irrelevant. Drawing out the practical experience and the practical solutions the Conscientious develops on a daily basis will be critical to your session's success. Ask them questions such as, "How have teams you belonged to solved such and such a problem?" or "What are a few ways you and your colleagues approach these types of challenges?" Help them by framing their response in terms of teams and groups.

As you prepare ahead of time, identify the types of personalities likely to be present, knowing which questions to ask for maximizing effective participation by all. With time and effort, you gain experience leading meetings with a diversity of group members and improve the meetings' chances of producing positive and productive results.

Chapter Four: The Nine Steps to Leading the Awesome

Now that you are through the introduction, it is time to get down to the strategy portion of the session. Below you will find the nine steps to creating an effective and practical strategic plan. Not all steps will be part of every planning session, though they should all be part of the final plan.

If your organization has already established and is satisfied with its values, mission and vision statements, you need not include a revision or replacement of them as part of the planning activities.

Step One: Documenting the Awesome

Originally step eight in this book's first draft, documenting the activities of your planning sessions and committee meetings needs to be step one. If you were to go through all of the session and committee work before reading this step, you might miss much of the value of the strategic planning process.

Before you start your planning session or committee meetings, let participants know that all notes and documents produced during the activities will be collected, saved, and used as resources for producing the final strategic plan. Then, ensure you have assigned someone to perform two critical functions.

First, bring a camera and take photos of the results from each activity in steps two through eight. This will include notepads at the tables, sticky notes on walls, and notes on wall posters.

Second, this person will also be responsible for collecting all notes produced by participants during the sessions and meetings. He or she will then promptly submit the materials and the photos to the executive officer, executive director, or executive committee.

These photos and notes can both help refresh the memory of whomever is assembling the final strategic plan report as well as serve to fill in any gaps that might appear in the final report.

Step Two: Prioritizing a Values Statement

Creating and posting a Values Statement provides staff, executives, board members and even external stakeholders with quick and clear instructions on how to act in any circumstance they are in related to the organization. More than a mere list of positive character traits, the Values Statement is a behavioral guide that prevents poor decision-making, empowers staff, and can even minimize the possibility of legal nightmares down the road.

First and foremost, values statements help the organization internally by establishing the foundation for appropriate decision-making. That said, they can also be used externally as a branding tool so current and potential customers will associate the stated values with your organization.

Despite the fact that a Values Statement lists just three to five core values your organization prioritizes above all others, creating the statement can be deceptively difficult. Not only must you work your way through myriad values to get to the core values defining what the organization truly stands for and which motivating values should be the basis of all difficult decisions the company makes, you must also keep the list to a minimum. Otherwise, you run the risk of creating a list too long to be memorable, thus ineffectual.

The following activity helps strategic planning participants to identify important values while also providing opportunities to explore unexpected priorities. It is called, "Values War," and it requires a set of Values War cards for each participant. Each set of twenty-five cards includes twenty that already have a value on them other organizations have selected as one of their corporate values, while five are blank to allow the participant to choose their own. Here are the directions:

- Divide the participants into groups of two (if there is an odd number of participants, one partnership may have three participants)
- Pass out ONE deck of Values War cards to EACH participant
- Give the group seven minutes so each participant can choose 10 of the values he or she believes is most important and central to the success and identity of the organization. If they do not find in the deck a value they want to include, they can write it on one of the blank cards.
- Have the participant set aside the remaining fifteen cards.
- Playing the game:

  The goal is to come up with five values upon which you and your partner can agree are most central to your organization's identity.

  1. Have the partners compare their ten chosen Values cards.
  2. Partners turn over the top card of their pile at the same time. If you both agree on the supremacy of one of the two values, place it in a shared "common values" pile. Otherwise, each partner places his or her values car in their own "War" pile.
  3. After going through all ten chosen values, if you still do not have five common values, take turns matching values from the "War" pile, accepting victory or defeat... both graciously, until you have agreed on five important organizational values.
  4. The partners write each of the five values on its own sticky note and place them on the board or wall, grouping them with similar values other partnerships may have placed on the board or wall already.
  5. Next, give one green, one yellow and one red sticky note to each participant and have them vote for the value they believe most represents their organization

(green), a value they would find acceptable (yellow) and a value they prefer to exclude from the Values Statement (red). To vote, they simply add the corresponding sticky note to their chosen values listed on the board or wall.

6. The three values with the most green sticky notes represent the most acceptable values to include in the Values Statement. Values with high numbers of yellow may also be acceptable. Values with large numbers of red sticky notes are deemed unacceptable to the group. In rare cases, some posted values with have similar numbers of green and red sticky notes, meaning there is a high level of tension within the group surrounding this value. As the facilitator, you may ask group members who voted green or red to share their thoughts or propose synonyms that might be more acceptable or less disagreeable. If no progress is made to minimize the tension, this value may not be one to include. Your organization wants values that all stakeholders will believe are important.

7. Finally, choose one to three wordsmiths* from the group to take fifteen minutes to convert the three values into actions.

    - They might consider adding, "Be," "Have," "Do" or "Spread" in front of the value, changing the value into an adjective as needed.
    - Example 1: Instead of "Kindness," "Spread Kindness" or "Multiply Kindness"
    - Example 2: Instead of "Expertise," "Expand expertise"
    - Example 3: Instead of "Integrity," "Do right"

8. Once the wordsmiths are done, have them report either to the group or to the executive and the board chair for final approval.

This is just one activity you can use to elicit input from all participants without making them feel you are trying to extract their molars. Still, it incorporates the right amount of stress to facilitate better decision making but not so much that it incapacitates the participants.

Forcefully forbid any wordsmithing during general planning sessions. It will stop the circulation of all creative juices and snap every creative bone in the collective body. The wordsmithing of statements and reports must be assigned to an individual or a small committee of two or three participants to address after the meetings are over.

Step Three: Identifying a Mission Statement

Many boards and organizational leaders jump right into the development of the organization's mission statement at the beginning of their strategic planning session. If the organization has never had a mission statement, this can be appropriate. Otherwise, updating or revisiting your organization's mission statement should come after you put together your Values Statement.

Mission statements have many uses. At the top of the list, mission statements identify the organization's purpose for existing, thus providing both direction and boundaries (even if adjustable) when considering current and future products, programs and projects.

For organizations seeking grants from government agencies or foundations, a powerful mission statement is necessary for successful fundraising.

Clients, customers and vendors also want to know what your organization does and why they should care. Mission statements provide this information.

To be useful, mission statements must be both memorable and repeatedly applied. Long and complex mission statements that never see the light of day beyond the initial strategic planning session completely waste the participants time. Even elegantly crafted statements that span three or four paragraphs will be ignored, whether on your website or on your lunchroom walls, by staff and clients alike. If it takes more than fifteen seconds to read, no one will want to expend the effort to figure out what your organization does. Mission statements need to be succinct but complete. Here are the three parts of a mission statement, each of which can range from one word to a five-word phrase:

1. Identify a problem or challenge (in the world, in the community, in the industry) needing to be addressed.
2. Provide an emotional reason for anyone to care about the problem.
3. Share what your organization does to solve the problem.

With these parts in place, a proper mission statement should be shared with staff, customers and the public just shy of the point of annoyance. If your mission statement is simple (clear), succinct (short) and compelling (gives the reader a reason to care), you should proudly display and promote it as often as possible.

Here are a few ideas for introducing others to your mission statement and reminding them of its importance:

1. Add it to the footer, header or sidebar of your letterhead
2. Add it to the email signature of every employee
3. Yes, post it in the lunchroom
4. Add it to your invoices, statements and receipts
5. Place it on your website on the "About Us" page

How do you get your participants to create or update your organization's mission statement? Consider the following activity or design a similar one to draw out the creative and practical skills of your participants. I call this activity, the Magic Wand:

1. Before beginning the activity, briefly and clearly share information about the value of mission statements, their purpose and their application.
2. Whether you use a template or create your own, provide each participant with a page that has the following questions on it:
    a. In 5-10 words, describe, what problem exists in the world that you hope your organization can help to solve:
    b. I would like to see this problem go away because I (e.g. am tired of..., can't stand to witness..., never again want to see...)
    c. A good way our organization can solve this problem is by...
3. Once the participant has completed this section of the activity form, they exchange it with another participant. Their next assignment is to condense their partner's response to statement "b" into five words or less. If they feel this is impossible, they can simply make a list of five related keywords.
4. Next, the participant condenses their partner's answer to statement "c" into five words or less. Again, if they cannot do this, they can just make a list of five keywords instead.

Once the participants have completed their assignments, they share their answers and the answers of their partner with a small group (two to four other participants). These small groups ask themselves these questions:

- Are these statements clear and concise?
- Do these statements align with the organization's identified values?
- Do the statements paint a mental picture?
- Are the statements engaging and inviting?
- Are the statements simple and memorable?

The small groups then prepare to share their results with the entire group. You may choose to have them share all responses (when there are few participants and time permits) or just their top two (when there are too many to share all). Direct or indirect feedback from the entire group can be used to narrow down the ideas into a few statements that the organization's wordsmith(s) can craft into viable mission statements.

Once the wordsmithing is done, you can either present the possibilities to the entire group for voting or to the executive committee for a final choice.

Once the mission statement is finalized, it must become part of the organization's day-to-day activities. Here are some ideas on what to do with your mission statement:

1. Place it on the company's "About Us" web page or a page dedicated specifically for the organization's guiding statements.
2. Introduce it to your employees, vendors, partners, funders and regulators. Explain in person, in writing or in a video how this mission statement identifies your organization's reason for being. Appropriate methods include emails, newsletters, blogs, and posters.
3. Include a review or reminder of your mission in your management meetings, staff meetings and future strategic planning meetings.
4. Work with marketing to discuss how to use your mission statement in your branding activities.

The best mission statements are simple, memorable, paint a positive mental image, and, above all, are used regularly by the organization's leadership management, its staff, and its marketing team to guide related decision-makers, from executives and sales to planning and compliance.

Step Four: Establishing a Vision Statement

Creating an organizational vision is one of the most confusing steps of strategic plans. You do not have to look very hard to find businesses (even big businesses) whose vision statement looks a lot like a mission statement, and vice versa. You can find other organizations whose vision statement goes on for two paragraphs, or worse, a page.

Vision statements are one-sentence declarations of what you hope your organization will have achieved or become three to five years from now. Vision statements steer the organization in the right direction. While Mission Statements can remain unchanged for decades or even the life of an organization, Vision Statements can and should change every time you go through a strategic planning session. If your organization is still holding to a vision from twenty years ago, your strategy is literally stuck in the past.

Your three- to five-year vision statement should answer these questions:

1. How do you hope your organization will have changed in 3 (or 5) years?
2. What major challenges do you hope to overcome by that time?
3. What accomplishments will indicate your success?
4. How do you want to be viewed or considered by your clients, end-users, vendors, and/or the general public?

During a planning session, expect to spend 30 to 60 minutes answering these questions. Using open-ended questions will rarely be your best option. Do not actually ask these questions of the group as a whole.

Instead, use activities that require the session participants to answer each question individually and, ideally, anonymously.

One example of such an activity is a game I call *Fruit Basket*. Each participant receives a sheet with the four questions on it. Sheets vary by the fruit on the top (e.g. Peach, Banana, Apple, Cherry). Sheets have four horizontal sections, each with one of four statements to complete:

1. Five years from now, life will be a bowl of CHERRIES because our organization will finally:
2. In spite of our best efforts, we will likely still face as our greatest challenge:
3. Still, we will know that we have succeeded because we will have:
4. We will surprise even ourselves by actually:

After completing the first statement, participants pass their sheet to another participant with the same "fruit sheet" who then completes the next statement before passing it again. By the end of the activity, each sheet will have input on the organization's five-year vision from four different participants.

Once each sheet is completed, ask each table (or group) to share the answers on the sheet they ended up with, rating sheets as "most likely to succeed," "most traditional," or "most original." Create additional categories of your own. Depending upon the size of your group, have each table choose just one sheet to share with the rest of the group in 3 minutes or less. What did the table like about the answers? Ask the group to listen for responses that resonate with participants. Once all answers have been read, post them on one section of a wall and have the participants vote for responses that they most appreciate (green sticky note), they find acceptable (yellow sticky note) and they would be highly resistant to (red sticky note).

At this point, you could dismiss the two or three wordsmiths for 15 minutes to work over the answers with the most green sticky notes in order to smooth out the ideas. Upon their return with three proposed versions, the group can again vote on each by using the green-yellow-red sticky notes.

Alternatively, the executive committee may instead choose to revisit the results and take additional input into account before making a final decision.

Step Five: Dividing the Vision into Annual Objectives

With your Vision Statement completed, your next step will be to develop one to three objectives for each year of your Vision. If your vision statement is a five-year plan, you will need one to three objectives for each of the five years.

Creating a Vision Statement is like deciding where you want to go on vacation. It can excite you and provide something to look forward to, but you need to break the Vision Statement down into objectives that give it more meaning. Sticking with the vacation analogy, once you have decided on a vacation destination, you will want to determine the types of things you want to do on your trip. You might want to "relax," "experience something new," "enjoy some views," and identify other general experiences you would like to include.

Objectives are not detailed plans but general statements of activities you would like to try. They note your hopes and aspirations for accomplishments, programs, campaigns, and projects that will help you fulfill your vision for the company.

Fleshing out your vision statement with annual objectives makes it more tangible and less touchy-feely. Annual objectives serve as expressions of optimism and hope that you will use later to generate a list of specific goals.

Even with these explanations, many executives, board members, and other organizational leaders will continue to struggle to differentiate between a Vision Statement, annual objectives, and annual goals. It will help to consider a list of words that you might use to establish three to five annual objectives. This list is by no means exhaustive, but it gives you an idea of how to proceed:

1. Acquire
2. Arrange
3. Attract
4. Augment
5. Balance
6. Become
7. Build
8. Conduct
9. Develop
10. Distribute
11. Enhance
12. Ensure
13. Establish
14. Expand
15. Extend
16. Find
17. Gain
18. Grow
19. Improve
20. Increase
21. Invest
22. Line Up
23. Maintain
24. Manage

25. Multiply	29. Raise	33. Set Up
26. Optimize	30. Reduce	34. Streamline
27. Partner	31. Reinforce	35. Support
28. Produce	32. Renew	

The Magnifying Glass Annual Objectives Activity

Distribute a list of sample objective starter words like the one above, with the Vision Statement available for all session participants to view. You might post the Vision Statement on the wall, project it on a screen, or print and distribute it for each participant to see.

Divide into groups of three to five participants for this activity. Give each group just 5 minutes or so to brainstorm individually as many objectives they feel must happen in order to achieve the established Vision. Participants write each of their ideas on a separate sticky note.

At the end of the brainstorming time, instruct the participants to place the sticky note with the objective they feel is most important on the wall (or perhaps on the Vision Statement itself if it is on a wall itself). Use the Eisenhower Decision Matrix (see example in Appendix) for this portion of the activity. The horizontal axis identifies the objective's urgency (left is not urgent and right is urgent). The vertical axis identifies the importance of the objective (top is important and bottom is not important). If the participant feels his or her sticky note objective is both important and urgent, they would place it in the top right portion of the matrix (whether the matrix is posted on a wall, written on a white board, or projected on a screen). If they feel it is important but not urgent, they would place it in the top left portion of the matrix, and so forth.

NOTE: keep in mind how high on a wall or white board participants may or may not be able to reach. Also, make sure to be aware of any participants who have vision or mobility issues that would prohibit them from participating in this or other activities.

Next, ask participants to pick one sticky note that does not belong to them and move it up, down, or side to side on the matrix depending upon the priority they feel it deserves.

Finally, give each participant the opportunity to move his or her original sticky note back to its original position with the understanding that her or she will give a 15- to 30-second justification of why the sticky note deserves to be located in its original position.

Be sure to take a picture of the resulting decisioning matrix. What remains on the wall may look like a visual mess, but it contains the objectives in prioritized order as the group believes they should be. The sticky notes in the top right become your top priority objectives, followed by those in the bottom right quadrant.

Sticky notes placed in the bottom right quadrant - urgent but not important - need to be reconsidered. If they are not important, you should consider how critical they are to your organization's success. Removing them or ignoring them may result from your discussion.

Finally, sticky notes found in the bottom left quadrant are unlikely to require much attention, as they are neither important nor urgent.

Step Six: Planting SEEDS™ (SMART Goals for the 21st Century)

For most strategic planning committees and groups, reviewing and developing a Values Statement, a Mission Statement, a Vision Statement, and annual objectives will take between eight and twelve hours (one to two sessions) with a professional facilitator. Without an experienced and empowered meeting facilitator, these first four steps can easily stretch through the end of the second day and even move into a third day.

Working on SEEDS™ goals, which require very detailed considerations, is best done at a sub-committee or small-team level. Once the main planning group has been divided into three to five sub-committees, schedule a day for those sub-committees to meet for another two to four hours each to set SEEDS goals for each objective and develop tactics for each of the SEEDS.

You have, no doubt, heard of SMART goals, but just as a refresher, the traditional version of a SMART goal means the goal must be Specific, Measurable, Achievable, Relevant and Time-bound.

If you look up SMART goals on Wikipedia or elsewhere, you will find scores of different versions. While I appreciate the value and power of SMART goals, what this variety means is there are too many individuals and organizations continuing to look for additional ways to improve their ability to achieve goals. After all, the best laid SMART goals of mice and men provide absolutely no benefit to anyone if they are not implemented.

For this very reason, I recommend SEEDS goals instead of SMART goals. SEEDS offer many of the same benefits of SMART goals with the additional requirements that you take ethical issues into consideration and that you share your goals in order to increase your likelihood of success.

SEEDS stands for:

Specific: A goal must be detailed and measurable.

Ethical: A goal must lead you along the higher ground. Otherwise, success will never provide lasting satisfaction.

Emotionally-connected: A goal must engage you and others emotionally in order to provide the necessary motivation.

Deadlined: A goal must be bound by due dates in order to create a sense of urgency and the capacity to measure progress..

Shared: A goal must be written, shared, and reported in order to increase exponentially your chances of success.

Let's look at each of these pieces of SEEDS goals in more detail.

SPECIFIC: When setting goals, you must make them very specific. You might consider starting with the objectives word list above and then drilling down into greater detail. Your SEEDS will not only answer the question What? but will also answer the question of How Much or How Many?

Consider the following examples:

Poorly-written goal: *We will improve customer service productivity to serve more customers.* This goal is vague and impossible to measure, nor does it answer how much or how many.

Mildly-better goal: *Customer service representatives will serve 10% more customers than last year.* While this sounds more specific, goals should not be percentage-based but based on hard figures.

Best goal: *Employees will successfully provide 4,500 satisfactory solutions based on customer surveys collection by December 31, 20XX.* This goal answers what will happen (provide solutions) while also answering both how many (4,500) and what type (satisfactory).

ETHICAL: Everywhere you turn, associations, accrediting organizations, educational programs and schools are integrating ethics courses into certifications, degrees, and continuing education activities. While most business owners have long attributed their success to the quality of honesty toward their clients, customers, vendors, and partners (see *Millionaire Mind* by Thomas Stanley, 2000), too many headlines over the past few decades have shone a spotlight on the natural, long-term consequences of unethical behavior in business.

When setting your specific goals, ask yourself if the goal is the right thing to do. Is it good not only for your organization but is it good for your employees, your partners, your customers, and your community? Settling for "no" to any of these questions is the sign of poor leadership.

If you approach your goals from the perspective of a zero-sum game (if you win, they lose, and if they win you lose), you are already skipping along the path, if not necessarily running down the middle, of the path toward unethical choices. While not all business decisions can end in a win-win scenario, leaders should start with this mindset from the beginning. Assume that your goals will automatically benefit all stakeholders and their communities.

EMOTIONALLY-CONNECTED: You must connect your detailed, ethical goals to an emotion that you feel in your gut. If there is no visceral connection, your heart will not be in your efforts, and if your heart is not in the effort, you will fail.

How do you turn a goal into an emotional hook? First, identify the possible outcomes that might take place if your goal fails. Such discussions often result in things that create fear, which is actually a powerful motivator. Fear, being fear, tends to be a very negative emotion. While it may be an important part of your discussion, fear should not be your primary emotional tie to the goal.

Turn your negative fear into a positive statement of home. Rather than saying, "We need to achieve ABC or we will all be out of a job by Christmas," you might restate it along the positive lines of, "Achieving ABC will generate X_1 in revenue to allow each employee X_2 in time for a Christmas bonus."

DEADLINED: Like SMART goals, SEEDS need to be time-bound. Whether the D stands for Deadlined, Deadlines, or Due Dates, the principle is the same: all important goals need to be tied to an end date in order to provide both a sense of coming urgency and accountability.

For goals whose deadlines are more than three or four months in the future, consider breaking your goals up into smaller and more immediate tasks. Goals should have components that can be measured on a weekly, monthly, quarterly, and annual basis.

SHARED: For generations, it has been assumed that you will be more likely to achieve your goal if you write them down. Some people credited a study from Yale back in the 50s, others a study from Princeton in the 70s. The reality, though, is that until 2015, no academy study had ever been done on the premise that writing goals down improves the likelihood of them being achieved.

In the mid-2010s, Dr. Gail Matthews at Dominican University in Northern California led a study[1] of hundreds of

---

[1] dominican.edu/academics/lae/undergraduate-programs/psych/faculty/assets-gail-matthews/researchsummary2.pdf

participants that not only confirmed that written goals are more likely to be achieved than unwritten ones but quantified the results. She found that participants who wrote down their goals were 42% more likely to achieve those goals than participants who did not write them down.

In fact, Dr. Matthews went beyond the original premise and found that two additional actions will have a similarly great effect on the accomplishments of goal writers: 1) Sharing their commitment to the goal with a friend and 2) Reporting regularly to your friend on your progress toward the goal.

Sharing your goals can be as simple as telling a friend about it or as "all in" as committing publicly to the goal on your social media pages. Participants who wrote down their goals and then shared them with a friend increased the likelihood of achieving those goals by 50%.

Finally, after writing down your goals and sharing them with a friend, you can all but guarantee the goals achievement by simply sending your friend(s) a report of your progress regularly. Such a form of accountability will increase the likelihood of completing your goals to 77% more than had you not ever written them down.

1) Write Down
2) Commit and Share
3) Report Regularly

Facilitating the Planting of SEEDS

Identify the top three to five prioritized objectives. Then, divide the session participants into three to five groups, and assign each one of the objectives.

Each group should have a sheet for each participant with the SEEDS acronym down the left-hand side of the page. Instruct the participants to take five to ten minutes to come up individually with as many goals for their assigned objective as possible. They will write the "Specific" portion of each goal on a sticky note.

Next, they place the sticky notes in the middle of the table for all group members to read. This is the "Planting" idea of the SEEDS. Group members spend a few minutes reviewing each of the sticky note goals and then vote for two that are not their own. You may want to provide small voting stickers to each participant.

The group then identifies the three goals that received the most votes and completes the rest of the SEEDS paper, briefly confirming the goal is specific enough, ethical, and emotional-based.

Finally, the group sets a deadline for the completion of the goal and decides who it would like to share (post internally, on social media, and/or on the website, etc.) and report on the goal (report to leadership, clients/customers, social and/or media connections, etc.).

If there appears to be too many SEEDS goals, you might consider sticking them to the wall and having participants use voting stickers to determine which to keep. One to three SEEDS goals per year of the Vision Statement is ideal.

Step Seven: Creating Tactical Plans

Tactics are the "how to" action plans that achieve goals. Because tactics tend to require specific assignments and day-by-day tasks to work on, small committees of three to six members much better fit the requirements than a general planning session.

Tactics might easily be confused with goals because they involve specifics and deadlines. However, tactics more appropriately align with approaches and mindsets than with goals. Tactics make up the step-by-step instructions that must be followed for the team to achieve their goals.

If you ever confuse tactics and strategies, consider this analogy from the Civil War. General Robert E. Lee was a master tactician. On a given battlefield, he was nigh impossible to beat or outmaneuver. General Ulysses S. Grant, on the other hand, was the master strategist, even though he gets much less credit nowadays than he deserves. Even though General Lee won battle after battle, Grant's strategy to destroy the south's ability to wage war eventually won the day.

Facilitating the Development of Tactics

When you assemble your committees, your objective will be to create tactical plans for each goal established previously. For meeting facilitators who love to be in the middle of the action, this part of strategic planning can be feel unfulfilling. Keep in mind that tactics require boots-on-the-ground knowledge, which is why membership in the committee should require direct experience with the SEEDS subject.

You have a few options on how to encourage and manage these activities. The key is having a visual for each SEEDS with a To Do list that includes the following:

- Refinement: Is the SEEDS specific enough? How can it be measured? When is the due date?
- Required resources: What are the resources necessary to achieve the goal? Resources include Human (staff, contracting, consulting), Financial, Physical (equipment and supplies), Intellectual (training, skills, knowledge), and Time
- Available resources
- Action Steps (1-3): Determine one to three steps that must happen in order to achieve the SEEDS goal. Answer questions such as: What needs to be done? Who needs to be involved (staff, contractor, consultant, customer, vendor, regulator, etc.)? What measurement will indicate success or completion? What is the estimated cost and when will financial support be required?

Find a sample Tactics Development Table in the Appendix

After the committee has completed its assignment (ideally within 24 to 48 hours), the executive officer or executive committee will then approve the results of the committee meetings and submit them for inclusion in the final report.

Step Eight: Assign Accountability

Now that the sub-committee has put together some detailed tactics for the SEEDS that, in turn, lead your organization to fulfilling its objectives and ultimately its vision and mission, you need to assign real people to ensure these tactics are both initiated and followed through.

The sub-committee makes the initial accountability assignments as part of their tactics development. The Tactics Development Table, in fact, has a question that assigns leadership responsibility for each step in the process of achieving SEEDS goals.

The executive officer, executive director or the management team, depending upon the size of the organization, then confirms those assignments or modifies them as necessary.

Step Nine: Implementing the System

Implementing the system plays THE central role in turning your strategic plan from a beautifully-crafted but never-used report into a guiding power that affects your organization's daily, weekly, monthly, and annual efforts, energies and success. This system requires only the following:

- *Commitment to follow through.* You, as the leader, must commit both to yourself and to your team. When committing to your team, replace words like "should" and "ought to" with "will." Make this commitment internally with yourself but also in both verbal and written forms for your leadership team.
- *Set Follow Up Prompts.* Virtually all organizational leaders have more computing power in the palm of their hands than NASA had in their control room when they landed astronauts on the moon. Still, we use our smartphones more for entertainment and communication than for business purposes. To incorporate your smartphone into your strategic plan, use your phone's built-in calendar or download a calendaring app. If you have never used your phone's calendar, do an Internet search for step-by-step instructions on setting up reminders, events, and meetings.

You need only set up six of these calendar prompts. Be sure to make them "recurring" reminders according to each meeting's frequency.

First, set a reminder every three to five years to gather your strategic planning committee in a full **_Strategic Planning Session_** (or sessions). Set the reminder to notify you about six months ahead of the time you want to hold the session(s), giving you time to gather and schedule your team, to look for a meeting facilitator, and to begin focusing your team on the upcoming event.

Next, set a meeting for twelve months later to hold your annual strategic planning re-evaluation session. Have the reminder notify you about two months ahead of time in order to schedule the majority of your planning team for a **_Strategic Plan Re-evaluation_** meeting. During this four- to six-hour meeting, you will address any necessary and major changes to your strategic plan.

Thirdly, set a calendar item for every three months from the time you adjourned your planning session. Schedule the reminder to notify you a month ahead of time so you can confirm with your leadership team their availability for this **_Strategic Planning Review_** session. During this one- to two-hour session, you will review the resources necessary for each team to complete their goals and SEEDS. You will also consider approving funding for necessary training, equipment, and other resources required by the teams to complete their assigned tasks.

The final calendar item you, as an executive, need to schedule is the **_Monthly Report_** with each individual manager or team leader. These are brief meetings, preferably in person, you hold with your individual leaders. Plan on the reports to last anywhere from fifteen minutes on the low end to 45 minutes in cases of extreme need. During these reports, you will mostly listen to your manager's or team leader's summary of their team's progress in achieving their tactics, SEEDS, and objectives. Note any resource needs that come up in order to bring them before the Strategic Planning Review committee or the executive committee for approval if necessary.

Help your management or leadership team set up their own reminders for the following two activities:

Your managers and/or team leaders will send you a brief **_Weekly Update_**, ideally via email although in person or even by text can work fine. Just make sure there is a paper or epaper trail of the discussion. The manager or team leader should spend no more than fifteen minutes assembling their update, which should require no more than five minutes of your time to read. If he or she is technically inclined, ask them to include progress line or bar charts to show patterns and progress. Because of these weekly updates, there should be no surprises during your Monthly Reports.

Finally, help your managers or team leaders develop the habit of holding a **_Daily Huddle_** with their small teams. Lasting just five to fifteen minutes, huddles should be held in a hallway, a corridor between offices, or perhaps an outdoor commons area. Make sure participants do not sit down or have access to chairs, since chairs will slow down the pace of the meeting and destroy the energy it needs. Huddles are not times to offer inspirational stories or provide staff recognition. Instead, the team leader asks his or her team members to briefly bring up any resources necessary to complete a SEEDS or tactic, asking other team members for help as needed. Team leaders should take information from the Huddles and use them to prepare their Weekly Updates to you. As a result, you should never be more than a week removed from urgent calls from your front line workers looking for help and support.

The third volume in the *Stress Less Strategy* series will address the follow up system in much greater detail. This system is so critical that it deserves its own book and materials.

47

Chapter Five: Conclusion

The nine-step strategic planning program from Chapter Four has the potential to change the trajectory of your organization. In its step-by-step format, it can take you from floundering or directionless to stable and consistent progression. My experiences with the strategic planning process prove to me they have the power to save businesses from lack of vision, hesitant or vacillating leadership, and even from themselves.

You care for few things in life more than your business (people are not things). As you consider and reconsider your next steps in improving and strengthening or redirecting and even redefining your business, commit to giving it the time and energy it needs.

Obviously, since you are reading this, you are at least considering a strategic planning session with your stakeholders. Remember that you will need to be actively involved, just as any other member of the team, in the planning and committee meetings. If you decide against using the services of a third-party facilitator, find an experienced meeting facilitator that can manage both your group and, frankly speaking, you.

Appendix

Mission Statement Formula

Create a simple and memorable working mission statement using the following formula.

To _____

Start with a verb then 5-10 words answering the question of why you exist

and
/ to _____

Start with an engaging verb then 5-10 words describing the positive difference you make in others' lives

Examples:

- *To organize the world's information and make it universally accessible and useful - Google 2020*
- *To pioneer the future in space exploration, scientific discovery, and aeronautics research - NASA 2006*

Key Principles

Reduce, Refine and Remember

- Make it concise. If you can't memorize it in 30 seconds, your staff never will.
- Use "visual" words that conjure emotional and compelling images (e.g. "pioneer")

Vision Statement Formula

While the Vision Statement Formula is straightforward, keep in mind that the vision is intended to describe what the future will look like if you succeed in fulfilling your mission. It should be succinct and inspiring.

Make a list of words that describe what you want your target clientele to look, feel, or act like if your mission succeeds:

_____

_____

_____

_____

Formula

Now, pick the most descriptive word from above and use it to describe your target clientele once you are successful.

A / Be
/ To /
We

_____

In 5-15 words, describe what your target clientele looks, feels, or acts like when your mission succeeds.

Examples:

- *A just world without poverty - Oxfam 2020*
- *We reach for new heights and reveal the unknown for the benefit of humankind - NASA 2020*
- *A better everyday life for many people - IKEA*
- *To make people happy - Disney (legacy statement)*
- *To help people and businesses throughout the world realize their full potential - Microsoft*
- *To make great products - Apple (2009)*

Annual Objectives Formula

Objectives are 2- to 4-word statements of aspiration for the year that move the organization toward its vision. You should have one to three objectives each year. Start your objective with a sweeping, generic statement of what you feel your organization needs to do within the following twelve months.

Acquire	Ensure	Manage
Attract	Grow	Optimize
Balance	Improve	Partner
Build	Increase	Produce
Create	Introduce	Rebuild
Develop	Invest	Reduce
Diversify	Maintain	Streamline

Create up to three Annual Objectives by choosing a verb from the list above and following it with what you think needs to happen:

1. _____

2. _____

3. _____

Examples:
- *Acquire more clients*
- *Diversity Our Staff*
- *Increase revenue*
- *Introduce higher quality products*
- *Rebuild our community image*

57

Planting SEEDS Checklist

SMART goals have been around since the early 1980s when the principles were introduced in a paper by George T. Duran published in *Management Review*. Originally an acronym for Specific, Measurable, Assignable, Realistic and Time-related, a more recent and popular version stands for Specific, Measurable, *Achievable*, *Relevant*, and Time-*bound*.

SEEDS, on the other hand, recognize developments in the business world and among the general population that enhance SMART goals. Use the following SEEDS checklist whenever you create a goal to maximize the likelihood of achieve your goals:

- ❑ *Specific*: Have you detailed the Whats, How Manys and How Muches of your goal?
- ❑ *Ethical*: Does your goal surpass mere acceptance and promote principled actions.
- ❑ *Emotion-drive*: Does your goal connect with people at an emotional level to inspire action?
- ❑ *Deadlined*: Is there a specific due date?
- ❑ *Shared*: Is your goal *written*? Have you *shared* it with someone or with a group? Are you reporting your *progress*?

Tactic Development Table

Committee Task	SEEDS #1
Refine -Who? -What? -How much or how many? -By when?	
Identify Required Resources -Human -Financial -Physical -Intellectual -Time	
Identify Available Resources -Human -Financial -Physical -Intellectual -Time	
Identify Resources Gap -Human -Financial -Physical -Intellectual -Time	
Establish Step #1 -What needs to be done? -Who needs to be involved? -What will be measured? -Who will lead the implementation? -What will it cost? When will finances be required?	
Repeat if Additional Steps Are Required	

Eisenhower Decisioning Matrix

All tasks related to your organization can be assigned values under two categories: first, its *importance*, and second, its *urgency*.

Important tasks are those required for success. Urgent tasks require action as soon as possible.

Tasks that are both Urgent AND Important should be your top priority tasks (1). Tasks that are Important but not Urgent should be second on your list of priorities (2). When considering tasks that are Urgent but not Important (3), discuss the potential consequences of removing them completely from your priorities list. Tasks that are neither Urgent OR Important (4) should probably be removed from your task list or simply ignored.

63

About the Author

Todd R. Christensen founded Todd R. Christensen Consulting in 2017 after seeing a need among the nonprofit and business communities for help with business meetings and effective strategic planning sessions. With over 16 years of facilitating more than 2,000 workshops for a nationwide nonprofit agency, Todd also holds a master's degree in international management with specializations in strategy and change management.

Todd is available to speak at conferences, to consult with business and nonprofit leaders, and to facilitate planning sessions, board meetings, leadership development and other gatherings.

Todd can be reached at Todd R. Christensen Consulting via www.ToddRChristensen.com, (208) 649-4788, Todd@ToddRChristensen.com or @trcconsultant.

www.ingramcontent.com/pod-product-compliance
Lightning Source LLC
Chambersburg PA
CBHW070316220526
45465CB00004B/1876